AF483644

Charlie's
Rules for Life

Hi, my name is Charlie! I'm a Cairn Terrier, a fierce but cute little dog.
I live at a boarding school in the Maryland countryside called Saint James.

My person is the "headmaster," or principal of the school, and I am the "mascot," which means I'm the important one!

Every year, during morning chapel, the headmaster gives a talk to the students of Saint James about me.

He tells them all about the good rules that I have taught him.

He calls his talk, "Charlie's Rules for Life," and he wrote this book to share my rules with you.

Some of these rules are easier for me than others, but they're all good rules, and I try my best to fol-low them.

Do you want to play?
Hi! My name is Charlie!
Do you have any treats?
Rule #1: Be friendly and say hello!

Rule #2: Every walk is an adventure!

Rule #3: Don't make mistakes in the house.

Rule #4: Not everything you want to play with is good for you...

Rule #5: Bark when you are lost.

SJS
Rule #6: Don't bark at cars!

MILK
Rule #7: The best toys are free!

Rule #8: Don't chase deer into the woods...

Rule #9: Don't pick fights with big dogs.

Rule #10: Love the one who feeds you.
CHARLIE
SJS

Rule #11: My leash works both ways! It connects me to my human and my human to me!

Rule #12: If you have nothing to do, you can always take a nap...

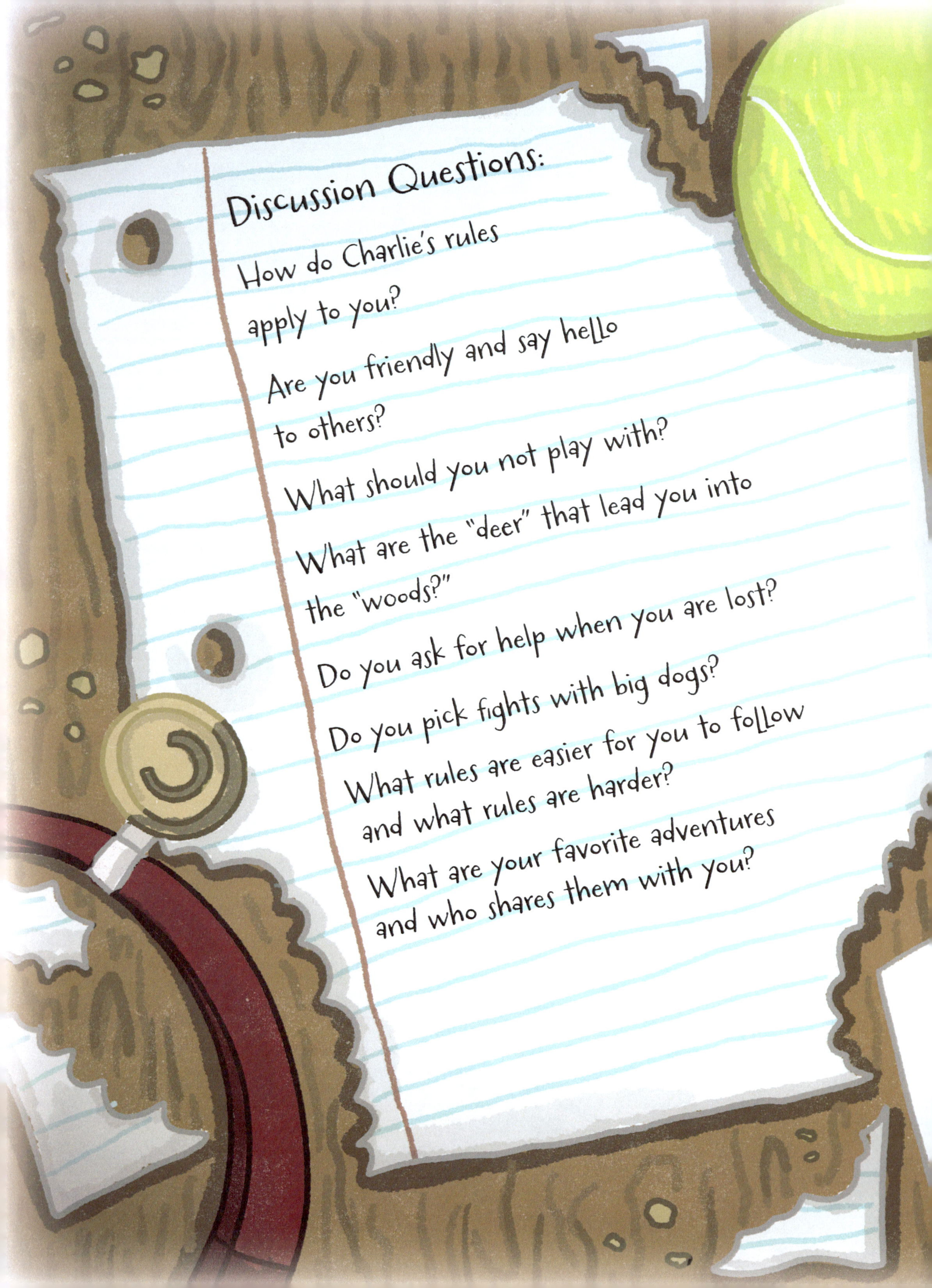

Discussion Questions:

How do Charlie's rules apply to you?

Are you friendly and say hello to others?

What should you not play with?

What are the "deer" that lead you into the "woods?"

Do you ask for help when you are lost?

Do you pick fights with big dogs?

What rules are easier for you to follow and what rules are harder?

What are your favorite adventures and who shares them with you?

Can you think of some other good rules everyone should follow, such as:
Tell the truth?
Be kind? Always try to help? Be brave? Be grateful?
Who are the people that your leash connects you to?
MILK
What are your "rules for life?"
Marching Charlie"

A Chapel Talk

The Revd. Dr. D. Stuart Dunnan
Saint James Chapel

As you all know, I was very fond of my big little dog Charlie, and we spent a great deal of time together over these past almost 17 years. During this time, he taught me some very important "rules for life," which I would annually share with you.

The first rule of life which Charlie taught me is to "be friendly and say hello." And this is a very important rule because one of the casualties of our modern "handheld" and "vidiot" age is our increasing lack of basic manners and our withdrawal from even casual interaction with others, who deserve our polite attention.

Simply put, it is rude to pass someone, especially someone who shares or is visiting our community, without saying hello and greeting them. It is also rude to make it somebody else's job to start the conversation. Charlie never did this! He always "said" an enthusiastic hello with confidence and cheerfulness with a big smile and a vigorous wag of his tail, which drew the immediate response "what a cute dog!" which he then used to his advantage. Clearly, we all need to learn from him and to always say a cheerful and friendly hello ourselves.

Charlie's second rule is "every walk is an adventure." He was always thrilled to take a walk, even when he was very old. He would bound out the door ready to see and smell new and fun things, to do "his business" in nature, to meet new people, and to check everything out.

For us also, every day is an adventure, which is why we should sing the hymn in chapel every morning to appreciate what God has given us, to engage and wake up! Each practice, game, and performance is its own adventure, even every class, quiz, paper, and test. If we are going to succeed and improve during the day and over the course of the week, we need to stay positive and embrace all our challenges, opportunities, and even our duties and tasks with enthusiasm, because we fail to live fully and diminish the experience of others when we don't. We limit the promise of our talents severely when we live passively with a negative, lazy, and self-centered approach to life, and we fail to find and create all the joy which awaits us.

Charlie's third rule is "don't make mistakes in the house." Impressively, Charlie figured out very early in his life when he was just a little puppy that he did not get to make up the rules for himself. Specifically, and most importantly for me, he could not do his business when he wanted to on the floor in our house. This was not always easy for him or convenient, but he paid attention to my consistent bribes and punishments and learned only to do his business outside. This was not his rule; this was my rule; but he followed it because he knew that it mattered to me – very much.

In the same way, we need to follow "the rules" too even though we may not always agree with them or like them in every situation or moment. Some rules come from the societies in which we work and live; some rules come from the government; some rules come from

God; and we do not have the "right" or the authority to choose which ones we are willing to follow. And these rules are not onerous or unreasonable. Indeed, all our rules here at Saint James can be condensed into four very reasonable expectations: be polite; be kind; be honest; and do no harm.

Charlie's fourth rule is "not everything that you want to play with is good for you." When we were out on an adventure especially after a rain in the evening, the toads came out, and he wanted to grab them because they were bite sized, bounced around, and squishy like his squeaky toys, but he learned early that they protected themselves with a chemical that caused him to gag. He still wanted to grab them, but he understood and remembered I think when I pulled him back.

As you are constantly reminded, teenagers can be particularly tempted to make the same mistake, and you know the list. Simply put, other people are not "things" to be played with, and some of the "things" we are tempted to play with, or others play with, are truly dangerous and potentially harmful to us and to anyone else we encourage to assume this risk with us.

Charlie's fifth rule is "bark when you are lost." When Charlie jumped into the upper pond beside our house as a puppy, he stood shivering in the cold water because he could not get out. He also stayed silent and waited for me to find and rescue him. This is typical of what he did when he got lost or trapped, and I used to think that he did this because he was embarrassed, but now I think that he did this because he did not feel safe and felt the need to hide.

We do the same thing and for the same reasons: we stay silent and do not ask for help when we need it, because we are too embarrassed or too afraid. So, like Charlie, we need to call out so that we can get the help that we need when we need it from those who can help us. And sometimes in your case, this would be the right adult – someone with the experience and the authority to help you, which is why I always ask you who are the adults whom you trust, because I need to know that you have someone, and hopefully more than one, whom you can confide in and reach out to when you need attention, assistance, and advice.

Charlie's sixth rule is "don't bark at cars." Charlie hated cars, although he loved to ride in them. I think that he was drawn to the moving tires and the sound of the engine, but he also did not like it when I was speaking to the driver through an open window and the car was stopped, because it looked too dangerous to him, like I was talking to "a monster." So, he went into "attack mode" and lunged at the car with the apparent expectation that he could grab the tire and wrestle the car to the ground.

This is of course ridiculous, but don't we do this too? Don't we also go after things that really aren't such a big deal and make a big fuss about something which we cannot control and is no real threat to us? Don't we also get upset when we really have no reason to be upset and create a lot of drama that might make us feel powerful and important in the moment, but does no actual good for ourselves or for anyone else?

And what would have happened if I had let go of his leash? He could have been hit by the car. And what happens to us when we fail to leash ourselves and to the others whom we involve? The false dramas that we create can do real harm.

Charlie's seventh rule is "the best toys are free." Two of Charlie's favorite toys were completely free: empty milk jugs which he loved to spin and chase, crush and destroy in the kitchen, and "lost" tennis and lacrosse balls which he "found" in the grass during our walks on campus. He loved to chase and chew them and roll on top of them to get a free massage.

Many teenagers feel the need to spend their parents' money to buy expensive "toys" that they do not need, and they love to "order out" to get the meal they particularly desire instead of the meal which someone has already prepared for them and is available for free – just to get exactly what they want when they want it. Obviously, this behavior, even if your parents can afford it, is entitled and spoilt. It can also be self-isolating and hurtful to those who do not have the disposable cash that you do. It is particularly sad when people who claim they have no money to give to others spend a great deal of money unnecessarily on themselves. Jesus has a great deal to say about this, which too many Christians ignore or forget.

Charlie's eighth rule is "don't chase deer into the woods." Charlie loved to chase deer, which again was ridiculous, as they were way too fast and too big for him, but he would follow them recklessly into the fields and into the woods, where he invariably got lost and I had to find and rescue him.

We can chase "deer" too. We can follow the wrong goals and seek the wrong prizes and get really lost when we do. Like Charlie, we often lack self-awareness, and we are not always willing to follow the right advice. We can take on more than we can handle and repeat the same foolish patterns over and over again. And when we chase these deer and get lost in these woods, we can only hope that others will find and help us, which can be dangerous for them. Think of all those people who refuse to leave their homes before a hurricane, expecting emergency responders to risk their lives during and after the storm to save them – really from themselves.

Charlie's ninth rule is "don't pick fights with big dogs." When he was a puppy, Charlie's best friend was Lizzie, Mr. Camp's Golden Retriever puppy, and they loved to wrestle and play together. Unfortunately, Lizzie was very nice and always let him win, so Charlie always thought that he could beat up big dogs, which of course he couldn't. Consequently, I needed to be careful that he behaved appropriately when he met a big dog, so that he did not get himself killed.

We can pick fights with "big dogs" too, with people in authority over us or just more powerful than we are. So, like Charlie, we need to be careful that we don't start fights that we cannot win, especially when the fight is avoidable. When it isn't, so be it, but usually it is, and it never pays to be overly self-confident or unnecessarily aggressive.

Charlie's tenth rule is "love the one who feeds you." Charlie loved me the best, which was grateful and smart on his part, but he loved my secretary Mrs. Davis more than me at lunchtime because she fed him fresh chicken by hand from her desk. He knew who counted, and we should too.

Teenagers especially can forget the sacrifices that their parents make for them and take their love and care for them for granted, treating them as their servants and acting like demanding brats. It is never a good look, and it isn't a good strategy either. The best strategy is to live a grateful life and to recognize all the good that others do for us, in your case, not just your parents, but your coaches and teachers as well. We also do well when we remember that "all good gifts come from above," so live our lives gratefully to God, fully aware that everything we "achieve" comes from the advantages, talents, and blessings that he has given us.

Charlie's eleventh rule is "my leash works both ways." When he was younger, Charlie used to pull on his leash and resent the ways that I was directing him and holding him back. But when he got older, he did not want to go on a walk without his leash to make sure that I was walking with him. The leash attached me to him and not just him to me.

This speaks to our own human relationships with those we love and who love us. Again, when we are younger, we sometimes resent the "leash" that connects us to our parents, but as we grow older, we discover that they are connected to us as well and need our help and support as we once needed theirs. This is true in our relationships with our teachers and friends as well. Love works both ways, not just one, and we walk in this life together only for the time that God has given us, so we should make the most of it, as Charlie did.

Charlie's twelfth rule is "if you have nothing to do, you can always take a nap." Charlie always loved his naps, and when he got older, he napped most of the time. One of our regular rituals on a Sunday afternoon was to nap together on my bed.

When I first arrived at Saint James, misbehaving students would often offer "I was bored" as an excuse for getting into trouble, but I am pleased that no one ever attempts to offer that reason now. My answer of course was and would be a simple one: "It is nobody's job to entertain you. It is your job to entertain yourself. And if you can't think of anything good to do, you can always take a nap." Churchill took a daily nap. Jesus napped. We all need to nap, especially when we are tired, as rest is healing for our bodies, minds, and souls. As Charlie taught us, we should nap more often, and this will help to keep us out of trouble.

I hope that these "rules for life' make sense to you and that you will adopt them as your own, as I have. Some are easier to follow than others, but they are all of them very helpful, centering, protecting, and worthwhile, and I personally am very grateful to Charlie for teaching them to me and for setting such a wonderful example of joy in life, gratitude, courage, forgiveness, resilience, loyalty, and affection for all of us to follow.

I have heard it argued that dogs can go to heaven because they have souls. We know this because they are capable of sacrificial love. I pray that this is true and that Charlie will be there to greet me just as he did every morning when we woke up and at the door in the evening when I was gone and he was waiting for me to come home.

Amen.

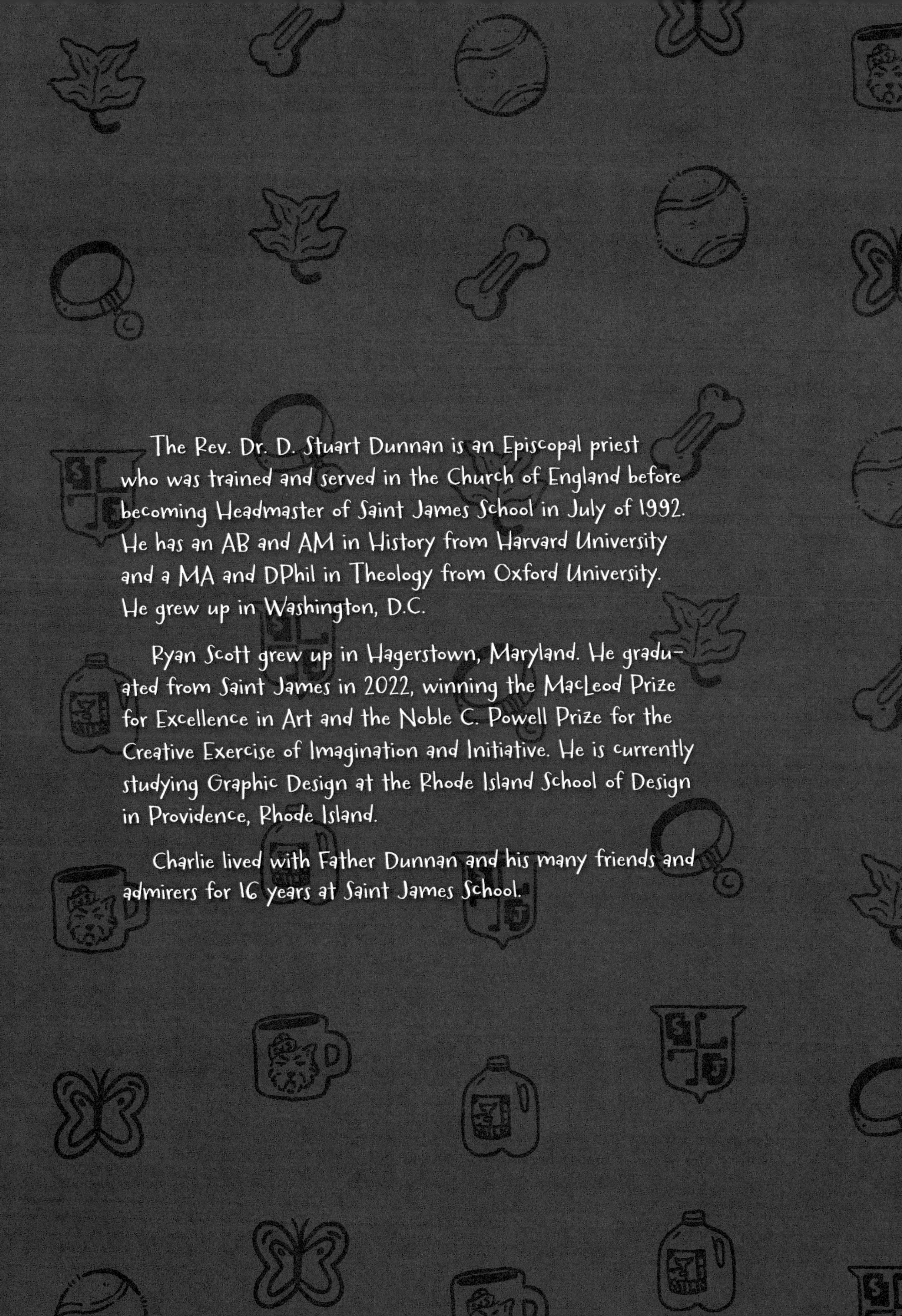

The Rev. Dr. D. Stuart Dunnan is an Episcopal priest who was trained and served in the Church of England before becoming Headmaster of Saint James School in July of 1992. He has an AB and AM in History from Harvard University and a MA and DPhil in Theology from Oxford University. He grew up in Washington, D.C.

Ryan Scott grew up in Hagerstown, Maryland. He graduated from Saint James in 2022, winning the MacLeod Prize for Excellence in Art and the Noble C. Powell Prize for the Creative Exercise of Imagination and Initiative. He is currently studying Graphic Design at the Rhode Island School of Design in Providence, Rhode Island.

Charlie lived with Father Dunnan and his many friends and admirers for 16 years at Saint James School.